Survival......I Totally Got This!

Epic survival skills for kids on everything from shark fighting to escaping quicksand.

Dale Jinks

Book Cover by Svitlana Stefaniuk and Illustrations by Author

1st edition 2024

About the author

Dale Jinks is a UK military survival, evasion, resistance to interrogation, and escape (SERE) instructor with 20 years of military experience in the Royal Air Force. More importantly, he is a family man, husband to Lucy, and proud father to his two beautiful kids, Sonny and Indy.

Dale believes that knowledge is power, and it's important to nurture a growth mindset in children as they mature into adults.

He founded the brand 'Surviving the Kids' to inspire children all over the world to go out and discover positive experiences and create lasting memories within nature.

For more books, blog articles, and information, visit the website at www.survivingthekids.com

FREE BONUS

A FREE GIFT JUST FOR YOU

As a special thank you for purchasing this book, you can download a FREE copy of our latest outdoor activity book by scanning the QR code above.

Contents

Disclaimer

This book has been written for the purposes of popular interest only. Although the guidance in this book has been written by an expert in survival techniques and practices, it should not be carried out without the supervision of experienced, knowledgeable and responsible adults present. The survival hacks and skills in this book are intended to entertain curious minds and to help promote safety at all times. Never carry out any method or technique described in this book without taking on further research and study in the specific field.

Above all else, always prioritize your safety and that of others.

Introduction

With the right mindset, we can't lose, we either practice what we've learned or we learn what we need to practice.

Noura, Philosopher

How tough are you? Do you know how to adapt quickly and overcome any emergency? Well, let's find out. This book is a detailed manual on surviving your worst possible day. What would you do if you got stuck in quicksand? Or what if you were face to face with a bear? Or shark? Could you light a fire using a battery and a stick of gum? Would you know how to survive an avalanche or a fall onto the subway tracks?

Planet Earth is a wonderfully wild and exciting place, but every now and then, we need to be able to deal with some pretty extraordinary situations, and sometimes these can be a matter of life and death. After more than four decades on this wild and wonderful planet and the last 20 of those years spent serving in the military, I have picked up some rather exciting and useful hacks that I felt compelled to tell you all about. This book is broken up into three different parts. The first part deals with ***'Ultimate Escapes'*** and how you can cheat death by knowing precisely what to do in extreme emergencies. The next part's full of my hand-picked ***'Incredible Survival Skills'*** designed to help you deal with anything life throws at you. Finally, the third section is your cheat book on overcoming the world's most ***'Extreme Environments'***.

At the end of each chapter is a survival axe rating, grading the skill or survival hack out of three for difficulty, usefulness, and coolness. That's just a guide; I'll let you judge for yourself.

I hope you find knowledge, inspiration, and, above all, enjoyment in the book. This is survival....and you got this!!

Ultimate Escapes - Life or Death

Survive a Crocodile Attack

How to escape the ultimate ambush predator

Large, semi-aquatic reptiles such as crocodiles, alligators and caimans belong to the Crocodilia order. They live in tropical and sub-tropical regions of the world, particularly around rivers and swamps. Most of the time, they are partly submerged in the water and can be very difficult to see from the land. If you know the area is 'croc territory', then stay at least 20ft away from the water's edge at all times. Camping or eating food close to the edge of the water is never a good idea in an area where crocs are known to be active.

Look – Your first line of defence against Crocodilia is to pay attention to and respect warning signs. However, signs where crocs live may not always be present, so be careful.

2. **Listen** – If you hear a hissing or rustling sound from the vegetation close to the water, get away quickly. There may be a croc hiding in there.

3. **Move slowly away**—If you spot a crocodile, keep calm and don't make any sudden movements; it may not have spotted you. Back away slowly.

If a croc charges at you, run away as fast as you can. Crocs are fast but only in short bursts, so you may be able to outrun it. If it does grab you, you should try hitting its eyes with your fists or jab them with your thumbs.

Keep fighting with all your might. If the crocodile tries to pull you under the water to perform its 'death roll,' take a big, deep breath before you go under and keep hitting and gouging those eyes as hard as you can.

Escaping Quicksand

Free yourself from this famous hidden danger

We have all seen the movies where the adventurous hero is hacking through a thick jungle when all of a sudden, SPLAT, they're waist-deep in quicksand and sinking fast. But unlike the movies, the chance that your head will sink completely under the surface is zero. You will probably sink to around waist depth and then be stuck firm.

Quicksand is a thick, dense mixture of clay, sand, and water. When disturbed, it becomes more like a liquid, and anything heavy on the surface can sink down. The more the quicksand is disturbed, the faster the object will sink. However, our bodies are not as dense as the quicksand, so it's impossible for us to sink entirely underneath the surface.

I'm stuck in quicksand – how do I escape?

It is extremely difficult to pull yourself out of quicksand without some help. The weight of the sand and clay makes it feel like your legs are in cement. You need to make some space around your legs and feet to allow water to flow into those areas, releasing some of that weight.

Wiggling your feet and legs can help, allowing you to slowly free up your legs one part at a time. Gradually, you can work your legs and body free from the quicksand using this method.

What helps is having something like a tree or rope to hold and pull as you try to waggle those legs free. It will take a long time, and it's important that you don't panic.

As we've already said, you will never be completely submerged in the quicksand. However, the danger exists on beaches where people may be stuck waist-deep in quicksand with the tide slowly rising! So be alert, and be careful where you put your feet!

HACK RATING

DIFFICULTY 

USEFULNESS 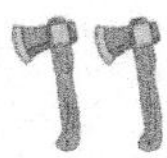

COOL FACTOR 

How to Survive an Avalanche

Be prepared for major trouble on the slopes

Activities like skiing and snowboarding can be tremendous fun. Fizzing down the alpine slopes at the speed of light is hazardous enough, but when you add the risk of a devastating avalanche, it pays to be well prepared.

Before you head out in the morning, always check the local weather conditions and take notice of any warning signs that indicate a high risk of avalanche in the area.

Be Prepared – Here are some handy things pack if you're in the mountains:

- **A phone** – Having a fully-charged phone in your pocket for contacting help is always worthwhile.

- **An avalanche transceiver or an emergency SOS beacon** – put this in a zip pocket close to your chest so you can grab it quickly.

- **A whistle hanging around your neck** – It's old-school, but a whistle is perfect for signalling help, and it will never lose its charge!

> **Did you know?** An avalanche can move downhill at speeds of over 80MPH, so trying to outrun it is not going to work.

So, if you find yourself standing in the path of a speeding avalanche, here are some of the most important actions you'll need to take in order to survive:

1. If there is absolutely no chance that you can get

out of the way of the avalanche path, then quickly look around for a solid, well-rooted object like a large tree or boulder. Hold on tightly to this until the avalanche has passed by. Removing skis, snowboards, or anything else that may cause you to be dragged away by the wave of snow is also a good idea.

2. An avalanche moves in a similar way to water, so try to 'swim' upwards with the wave to keep your body as high as possible. Try to keep your face and mouth facing up towards the sky.

3. If you become buried by the snow, you MUST remain calm. Clear some of the snow away from around your nose and mouth so you can breathe easier. Lack of oxygen is more dangerous than the cold snow at this point.

4. Tumbling down the mountainside in a thick blanket of snow will certainly flip you around a lot, and it's difficult to dig your way out if you don't know which way is up. Gravity will always pull it downwards if you slowly dribble spit from your mouth. Start digging in the other direction!

5. Use whatever you have with you to start signalling rescuers for help. Hit the red button on your SOS beacon, blow your whistle, or shout at the top of

your lungs.

Around the world, most avalanches are triggered by a person skiing or moving through an unsafe area. To reduce your risk of getting caught by an avalanche, beware of steep slopes with no trees or rocks on them, hollow-sounding snow, or recent heavy snowfall conditions.

HACK RATING

DIFFICULTY 

USEFULNESS 

COOL FACTOR 

How to Deal With a Shark

Forget jaws, it's just mistaken identity

Although your chances of being attacked by a shark are extremely small, you should always treat the ocean respectfully and cautiously. Always remember that you are a guest in the habitat of many amazing creatures who are happily going about their everyday aquatic business. From under the water, our movements and shape look similar to the shark's natural prey – fish and seals. When sharks do take a bite out of a human, it's a case of mistaken identity. Generally, they will realise this right away and leave you alone after that first bite.

Before heading out to enjoy the surf or cooling waters, check beach signs and notices, and always be sure to stay inside the bathing nets if they are in place. It is not a good idea to swim in the ocean if you have a cut or wound that's bleeding, as sharks could be attracted by this.

Sharks are sophisticated predators, and they will normally surprise attack their prey from below. However, if you notice a shark close by, it's important not to panic. Slowly and calmly move to the safety of shallow water, keeping your eyes on it as you do. Do not splash or thrash around in the water; this will make the shark more interested in you and more likely to attack.

If the shark does rush towards you, you will have to try and defend yourself. The best way to do this is to kick, punch and claw at the shark's weak or sensitive areas, which are:

1. **The gills**
2. **The eyes**
3. **The snout or tip of the nose**

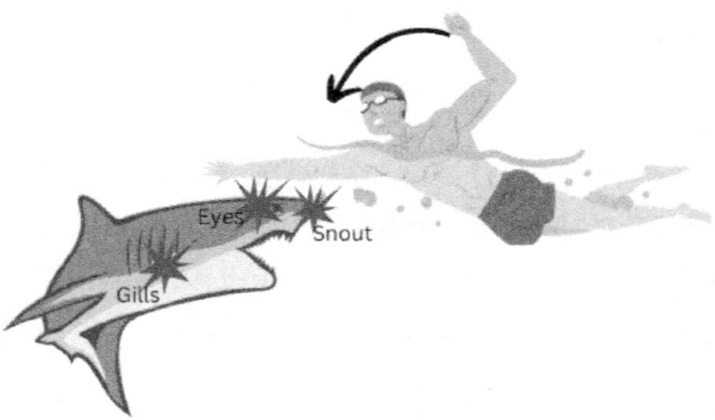

This may be enough to get rid of the shark, but if it does decide to take a bite, keep aiming for those sensitive areas we mentioned above and shouting as loud as you can for help.

Sharks are not out to get us, despite what some movies will tell you! But if a hungry shark ever mistakes you for a young seal, use the guide here and live to tell the tale.

HACK RATING

DIFFICULTY

USEFULNESS

COOL FACTOR

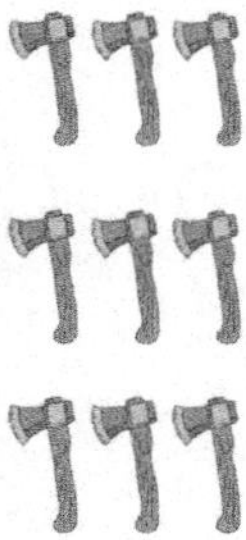

Face to Face With a Bear!!

What should you do if you bump into a bear in the wild?

Animal encounters are part of the deal whenever you're exploring or hiking in the wild. Most of the time, we're not even aware of the presence of animals around us. Most animals, such as deer or rabbits, will hear, smell or see us coming and probably hide until we have passed by. But sometimes, if we catch an animal by surprise and it feels threatened, or even worse, it feels their young could be in danger, they can react dangerously.

Large mammals like bears are very protective of their young cubs and are prepared to dish out pain on anything, or anyone they feel might be a threat. If you are going to be moving around in a region where you know bears could be, then you should always carry some bear spray and something that will make a loud noise.

1. If you spot a bear, the most important thing to do

is to STAY CALM. Don't look the bear directly in the eyes, and move slowly to ready your bear spray if you have it.

2. Make yourself as large and tall as possible, even standing on tip toes! If in a group, all huddle together to form one single mass. Keep the bear at a distance and slowly move away, but you must never run. The bear will see this as an invitation to give chase, as they're faster than you!

3. If the bear does decide to come towards you, wave your arms and make as much noise as you can by shouting something like "HEY BEAR!!" to see if you can scare it away. If this fails and the bear looks like it wants to attack, DO NOT RUN. Face the bear and use your spray, or throw anything you have with you towards it.

4. If the bear still decides to attack, then what happens next depends on what type of bear you're dealing with. If it's a black bear, then fight with everything you have by hitting the bear around the nose and eyes. If it's a brown bear, which is generally much larger, then the best thing to do is play dead. Lie face down and hope the bear decides to leave you alone.

HACK RATING

DIFFICULTY 

USEFULNESS 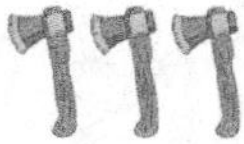

COOL FACTOR 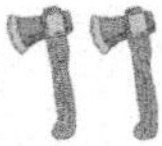

How to Survive a Wildfire

Learn how to escape a raging forest fire

As our summers become hotter and drier each year, the chances of being caught up in a terrifying wildfire increase. In drought conditions, the slightest spark can quickly become a sweeping inferno, moving up to 15mph and destroying anything in its path.

To make sure you're not the one responsible for causing a wildfire, always take your time to put out a campfire fully, dousing the ashes with water if possible. Before venturing out, check for local warnings on the news and nearby signs. If there is any doubt, it's better not to risk it.

However, sometimes you can just be plain unlucky, so here's what you must do to escape a wildfire:

Be alert – Notice signs of fire like the faint smell of smoke, a crackling sound in the distance and clouds of smoke or falling ash.

Cross a river or natural fire break – Fire needs fuel to grow and spread, so head for an area that a fire cannot move across quickly, such as a body of water, a clearing in the forest or a road.

Get low – If you find yourself trapped by the fire, get as low to the ground as possible. Find a ditch or dig down into damp soil if you can before lying face down with your head facing away from the approaching flames. Cover yourself with dirt or wet clothing and hold your breath as the fire moves over you.

HACK RATING

DIFFICULTY 

USEFULNESS 

COOL FACTOR 

Escaping From Cable Tie Handcuffs

Harness your inner Houdini with this handy life skill

Any secret agent worth their salt is trained to defeat cable tie handcuffs if captured by the bad guys. That's just a fact. Unfortunately, we're not all trained secret agents like Jason Bourne or James Bond. So what would you do if you needed to break out of some plastic zip-tie handcuffs? Well, in this chapter, you're going to find out.

It's actually remarkably easy to pick the cable tie mechanism; you need something thin and sharp, like a safety pin or a straightened-out paper clip.

A cable tie works using a ratchet system that allows it to be tightened easily but does not release and loosen off. A small lever inside the mechanism (the cube bit) pushes down into the 'teeth' or lines on the cable tie, stopping any reverse movement. So, all we need to do is figure out how to lift this small lever away from the teeth of the cable tie to release the simple ratchet mechanism and loosen it off.

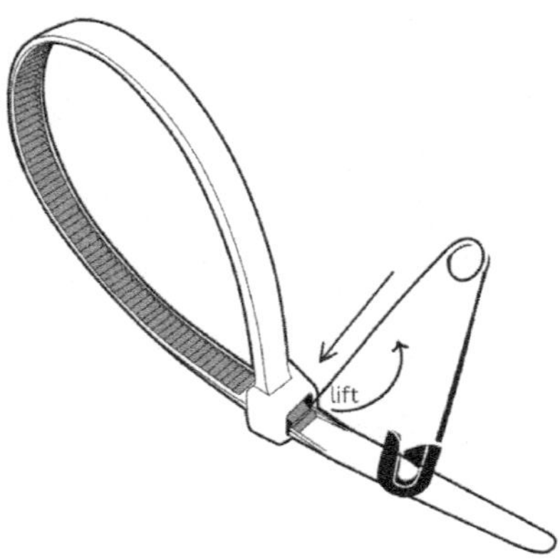

1. Press the needle into the gap at the side of the lever sitting on the teeth.

2. Carefully lift and prize the lever up and away from the teeth.

3. Once the lever is clear of the teeth, you can open the cable tie

You need to wait until you're handcuffed to try this out. Before you or someone you know cuts a cable tie at home, see if you can pick the mechanism and release it without needing to cut it. You'll look like a secret agent, but also you can reuse that cable tie for another job around the home.

HACK RATING

DIFFICULTY 

USEFULNESS 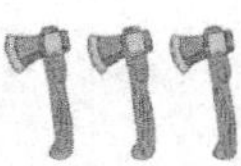

COOL FACTOR 

How to Survive a Snake Bite

The immediate first aid drill that may save your life

A bite from a venomous snake can be deadly, depending on the type of snake and the age/size of the unfortunate person who is bitten. Nobody goes out looking to get bitten by a snake, but moving through desert or woodland wilderness areas sometimes means we cross paths with these misunderstood reptiles. Snakes are not looking to bite the first human they see; in fact, they are most certainly more afraid of you than you are of it. Most of the time, when a person suffers a snake bite, it is because they have surprised the snake by walking up to or on top of it before the snake has had a chance to slither away into the undergrowth.

According to the World Health Organization, **nearly 3 million people are bitten by venomous snakes worldwide every year**. In the world, India has the highest number of deaths from venomous snake bites each year.

Here are some of the signs and symptoms you might see from a venomous snake bite:

- Two puncture wounds at the wound (made by the snake's fangs!!).
- Redness and swelling around the bite.
- Extreme pain and tenderness around the bite.
- Vomiting and dizziness.
- Twitching muscles and a tingling feeling in the face and limbs

Fact – Even if a snake's head is chopped off, it can still bite you!

Snake Bite – Basic First Aid

1. You probably need anti-venom to prevent your symptoms from worsening, so call the emergency services immediately. Don't wait to see if things improve later. The sooner you receive antivenom, the better your chance of avoiding permanent damage.

2. Keep calm, as frantically panicking will not help your situation. You need to think clearly, especially if you're alone.

3. Lay or sit down and remove any rings or tight-fitting clothing before the swelling kicks in.

4. Note the type of snake that bit you. Even if you can give the emergency services a simple description, this will help ensure you get the best treatment and correct antivenom.

DO NOT.........

- Use a tourniquet or similar to reduce blood flow to the bitten limb.

- Wait to see if it's bad – get help right away!
- Try to cut or suck out the venom. This will not help at all.
- Try to catch the snake to show emergency services. You risk getting hit with even more venom and making things worse.

Following these simple tips could prove life-saving if you or someone you're with is unfortunate enough to suffer a bite from a rattlesnake or other type of venomous snake.

HACK RATING

DIFFICULTY 

USEFULNESS 

COOL FACTOR 

Survive a Piranha Attack

Avoid being a snack for the world most terrifying small fish!

The most ferocious and dangerous species of piranha is the red-bellied piranha of South America. They swim around the great waterways of the Amazon basin in large groups, waiting for the familiar scent of blood or the sound of thrashing in the water nearby. Like sharks, either of these sounds is like ringing a dinner bell to a school of hungry red-bellied piranhas.

Although most of the developed world has grown to fear the very word piranha, the tribes that live alongside this interesting creature in the Amazon rainforest actually go out in search of them. That's because piranha is among the most tasty species of fish in the world. However, local fishermen know the dangers that these little guys can pose. In fact, in 2013 in Argentina, 70 people were bitten by a frenzied group of angry piranha during one single attack as bathers cooled off in the river during a hot summer day. Luckily, nobody lost their life that day, but one little girl did lose part of a finger!

Although rare, piranha fish have attacked people, and it's important to know how to avoid an unpleasant encounter with these tiny, sharp-toothed swimmers.

How to avoid a piranha attack:

- Do not enter a river or lake with open wounds or cuts. This seems obvious anyway due to the risk of infection, but you should never go swimming if you have a bleeding wound. This can act like bait to meat-eating predators like the piranha.

- Don't swim near to people who are fishing. It is easy for a piranha to mistake your toe or finger for the bait. The fishermen often 'chum' the water with meat and blood to attract these snappy fish.

- Don't thrash around when in the water. Like sharks, piranhas are attracted to sounds that they think may be a smaller fish in distress and an easy meal.

- Don't swim during a dry season. Food is scarce for these fish during a dry season, so fish like piranha may be tempted to try a new and different food than what they normally choose—you!

What if you get attacked:

- Get out of the water immediately. A piranha attack works by just one fish biting the suspected prey. If the prey does not respond or appear threatening, the rest of the school jumps in on the action, and a feeding frenzy takes place.

- Alert everyone around you. Make sure other bathers around you know what's happening; otherwise, the hungry school may move on to another nearby victim.

- Assess the bite and get first aid. Check the bite area once you're out of the water and safely on dry land again. If you're bleeding, find a bandage or piece of clothing that you can tie tightly around the area until you can get medical assistance.

Piranha attacks on humans in the Amazon are very rare, with around 200 reported cases each year, mostly resulting in only minor injuries from single bites. Despite this, you should always use caution and best judgment when moving through waterways in areas where piranha fish are known to live and hunt.

HACK RATING

DIFFICULTY 

USEFULNESS 

COOL FACTOR 

How to Survive a Lightning Strike

Avoid injury or worse by following these simple tips

If you hear thunder when you're outside, the best thing to do is get indoors as quickly as possible. Buildings offer great protection from lightning strikes, as they contain pipes and wires that help safely transfer any potential strike into the ground. If you can't immediately get indoors, a large vehicle like a car or truck is also a great place to safely wait out the storm.

The worst-case scenario is you have no vehicle or building to escape to. If this is the case, you should find a low area like a valley or ravine to wait, as generally, the higher you are, the more chance there is of being struck by lightning. Get away from areas of water such as lakes and rivers, as water is a conductor of electricity. Stay clear of large trees, and certainly do not take cover below them. Trees are tall and, therefore, are commonly hit by bolts of lightning.

Signs that a lightning strike is about to happen;

- The hairs on your head and body suddenly stand on end.
- Your skin begins to tingle
- You hear a hissing or crackling sound
- Metal objects around you begin to glow blue/white

If you are outside in the open and notice any of these signs during a thunderstorm, doing the following things will greatly increase your chances of survival if you are struck by lightning:

- Crouch down as low as possible, with only the balls of your feet touching the ground. You should look like a catcher, ready to receive a baseball.

- Touch your heels together, allowing electricity to pass in one foot and straight out of the other if you're hit.

- Cover your ears with your hands to protect them from any loud thunderclaps that may occur nearby.

- Do not touch anything metal that will conduct electricity.

Now you know how to react in a lightning storm and how to give yourself the best chance of survival if you are one of the hundreds of unlucky people who get struck by lightning each year.

HACK RATING

DIFFICULTY

USEFULNESS

COOL FACTOR

How to Break Down a Door

Trapped and need to escape a room?....this is what you need to do.

You've seen this many times in the movies: the hero delivers one well-placed kick, and the door bursts open, almost flying completely off its hinges. In reality, the task of breaking down a door can be difficult, and much will depend on which direction the door opens.

If you're trapped in a room and the door opens by swinging away from you, then you're in luck. This is the easiest type of door to bust open using a forceful kick. However, if the door opens by swinging in towards you, it will be almost impossible to break through using this method.

The easiest way of working out which way the door opens is to look for the hinges. If you can't see any hinges, then it likely means that this door opens by swinging away from you; this is good news if you're trapped! However, if the hinges are on the same side of the door as you, then it probably swings open towards you, bad luck.

In our case, we can't see the hinges, so we're confident the door will open away from us. Here's what you need to do:

1. First of all, do not charge at the door with your shoulder like on TV. This method is more likely to dislocate your shoulder than burst open the door.

2. Find the lock mechanism. It's usually below the door handle, where the keyhole is. This is the weakest part of the door.

3. With a powerful front kick and using your body weight, drive the heel of your foot right into the part of the door closest to the locking mechanism.

4. It may take a few attempts to open, so keep going until the wood around the lock splits away com-

pletely and the door swings open.

You may think that performing your very best flying kung fu kick into the door will do the trick. However, don't be tempted to try this, as it will make you less balanced and stable; you'll also end up with less power in the kick.

Don't practice this at home, as I'm sure your parents will not be too pleased to find broken doors throughout the house.

HACK RATING

DIFFICULTY 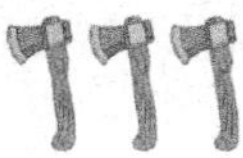

USEFULNESS 

COOL FACTOR 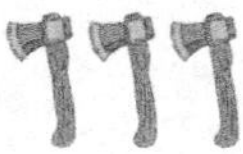

Build the Most Effective Smoke Signal, Ever

You'll be found in no time with this brilliant survival hack

Finding a person in a remote wilderness can be like finding a needle in a haystack. You need to take charge of the situation and help the rescue party by thinking smart and making yourself hard to miss. First, you need to 'ATTRACT' the attention of anyone who may be close enough to help. Then you will want to 'FIX' that attention so they want to investigate further. Then, once you're at this stage, you need to 'LEAD' that person right into your location.

Sending smoke high into the air is an excellent way to signal to anyone around that you need help. It can take rescue forces days and even weeks to find someone in a large wilderness area, especially jungle or forest mountains, where it's impossible to see through the thick tree canopy.

A smart survivor will build a signal fire, which can be lit quickly once they hear a plane or helicopter passing overhead. The plumes of thick, black smoke billowing into the air above the trees are like turning on a huge neon sign above your head saying, 'I'M RIGHT HERE!!!'

The Tripod Signal Fire

This method of building a signal fire is military-trusted due to its quick burn rate and 'thermal punch' effect, pushing a thick smoke column high into the sky.

- The **tripod** consists of 3 long, straight branches

around 4-6 feet long, depending on how high you want the signal fire. You lash these together with some cordage or tree roots.

- The **shelf** consists of a few twigs and small branches spread across the inside of the tripod legs. This is what the dry tinder and thin, snappy kindling will sit on, ready to burst into a towering inferno of flames once lit.

- The **green mushroom cap** is the finishing touch but is super important. This layer of thick, green vegetation is what gives your signal fire the plumes of thick black smoke. Lay these over the top of your tripod.

Light the tinder on the shelf to ignite your awesome signal fire, and watch as the kindling above quickly burns, setting light to the green material sitting on top. Within 120 seconds, you should have a column of thick black smoke punching high into the sky above, making sure the rescue party has no doubt where you are!

HACK RATING

DIFFICULTY 

USEFULNESS 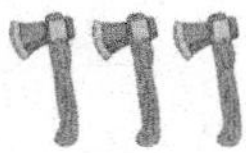

COOL FACTOR 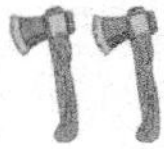

Signalling to Aircraft....I NEED HELP!!

How to build the ultimate signal device

The most efficient way for a rescue party to search for somebody lost in the wilderness is by air. Therefore, it's important that you make yourself known to helicopters and low-flying planes using a **Ground-to-air signal**, or G-TAS for short. This technique is taught in the military during survival training and has proved very effective in many real-life survival situations. A G-TAS is a large symbol or shape that the survivor builds in an open area and is usually a 'V' shape or even the word 'HELP' or 'SOS. It is important to make it obvious that someone here needs help.

To be seen from the air, it is important to ask yourself these questions when building a G-TAS:

- **Can my signal be seen?** Build your signal in a clearing so it can be seen easily, rather than inside a thick, dense wood or somewhere that can't be seen from above.

- **What will catch the eye?** Making obvious straight lines that look out of place is a great start. As we know, straight lines do not exist in nature and always look man-made or deliberate. Using bright colours and shiny objects is also a great way to catch the eye.

- **Can I stay close to my signal?** You want to be as close to your G-TAS as possible, as this is the first place the search party will look. If it's safe to do so, stay near your signal and wait for rescue.

Your G-TAS should be 6 metres long and 1 metre thick. If you can't build one that big, then make it 3 metres x 0.5 metres. The ratio is important because satellites and other technology are very good at quickly searching large areas for objects of a specific size and shape. Use things that are around you, like logs, branches and bright vegetation, to create straight lines and contrast that will catch the eye.

You are trying to:

ATTRACT someone's eye

FIX their attention long enough to investigate

LEAD the rescue party to where you are

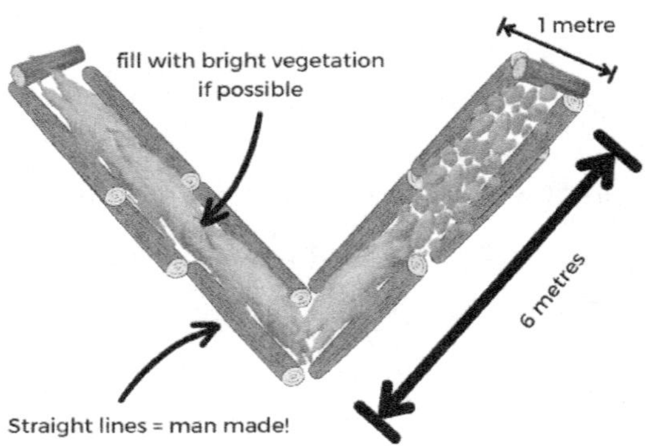

A Ground-to-Air Signal is a great way of showing passing aircraft where you are if you find yourself lost and in desperate need of help. The rules are simple...make it big, with straight lines, and fill it with bright, contrasting colours!

HACK RATING

DIFFICULTY 

USEFULNESS 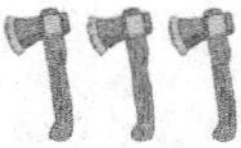

COOL FACTOR 

Incredible Survival Skills You NEED to Know

Turn a Battery Into a Fire Starter!

How can an everyday battery be used to help start fire in a survival situation?

Imagine the situation, you are out hiking in the wilderness and after a while find yourself hopelessly lost. Every step you take feels like it's just making matters worse. It's getting cold and daylight is disappearing by the second. So you decide to stop and make camp for the night. As it's cold, you collect some dry tinder and firewood, when you suddenly think to yourself – heck! I've forgotten my trusty lighter. Now what?!

Fortunately, you have a stick of gum in your jacket pocket and a head torch in your backpack. Here is what you need to do.........

Remove the batteries from your head torch and set them aside for now. Now find that stick of gum and carefully remove the foil wrapper, but DON'T screw it up and throw it away! You will need this. Now pop the gum into your mouth and chew, the minty juiciness will hopefully distract you from the fact you're lost.

Tear the long edges of the foil wrapper to create an hourglass shape where the thinnest part is in the middle. This should be as thin as you can make it without it breaking.

Now, all you need to do is touch each wide end of the foil to the positive and negative terminals of the battery. This makes an 'electrical short' at the thin part of the foil wrapper and creates enough heat to ignite a pile of tinder. Cotton wool works superbly, but dry grass or wood shavings work well, too.). Once the tinder pile is alight, then gradually add more fuel to create the perfect campfire. If not enough heat is being created to start your fire, then you may need to make the thin part even thinner. This will even work if the foil snaps; lightly touch the two thin ends together to create the short.

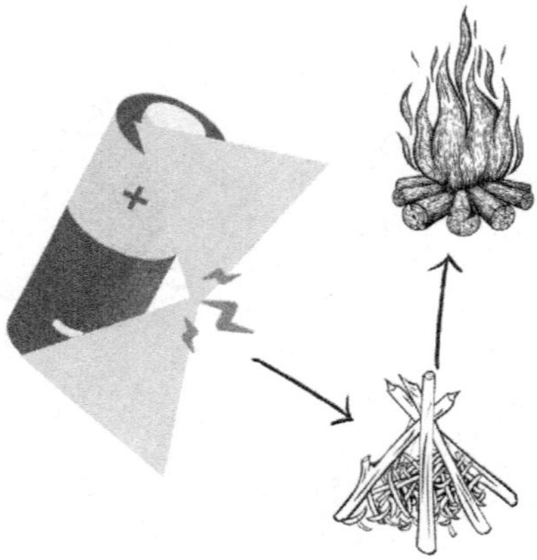

There it is: Make a fire using a battery and a piece of foil paper. This is a fantastic survival hack for when you've left your lighter at home.

HACK RATING

DIFFICULTY 

USEFULNESS 

COOL FACTOR 

Crayon Super Candles

How to use an ordinary wax crayon as an emergency candle.

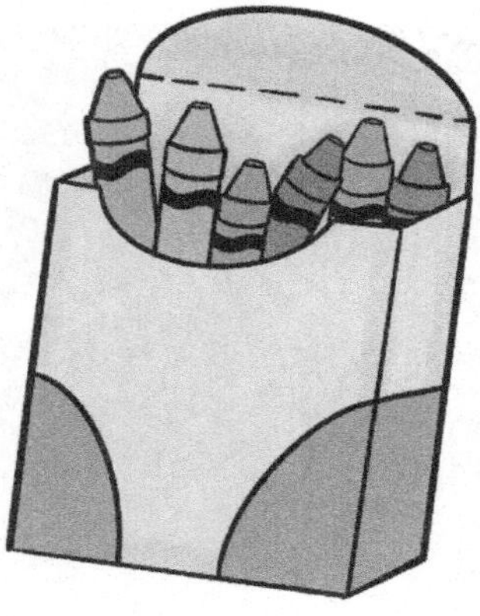

Candles are incredibly useful items to have with you when camping or hiking. They can hold a flame for long periods and were the first edition of a light bulb, lighting up mud huts and castles long before electricity was around. Candles are also great for boosting a struggling campfire, acting like a lighter when used to introduce extra heat into burning embers.

Did you know that the same wax crayons we use to create amazing artwork and colourful pictures also make fantastic emergency candles? That's because they are made from wax, similar to normal candles, and contain highly flammable paraffin. The paper around the crayon acts like a wick, taking the initial flame and continuing to burn bright as the wax around it melts.

If you want to give it a try, find an adult first to help make sure everything is safe. To light your crayon candle, snip off the pointy tip of your crayon level with the paper. Then, melt the bottom of the crayon using a flame for a couple of seconds and stick it down onto a flat metal surface. Then hold a flame to the cut end until the crayon lights, this may take 5-10 seconds. Once it's lit, the crayon should burn with a big bright flame for around 15 minutes.

HACK RATING

DIFFICULTY 

USEFULNESS 

COOL FACTOR 

Turn a T-shirt into an Arm Sling

The genius quick-fix to protect a badly hurt arm

Any time you are exploring tough terrain, such as winding mountain paths or steep valleys, there is a risk of injury. Sometimes this is just a bruised ego when you slip over in the mud and end up on your butt. However, when losing their footing, most people will throw their arms out to cushion a fall. Often, this can result in sprained wrists, jolted shoulder joints, or even a broken collarbone. If this happens and medical attention is not close by, then a great tool you can use to help keep the arm comfortable and support the injury is to make a T-Shirt Arm Sling.

To make an arm sling using only a T-shirt:

1. Grab a T-shirt from your bag or a person in your group. Roll the shirt up to make a cloth hoop around the neck hole.

2. Place your head or the casualty's head through the neck hole, wearing the shirt like a necklace.

3. Place the injured arm up through the bottom of the shirt and into the arm hole on the opposite side. Pull the rest of the fabric down over the elbow to secure the arm in place.

4. The T-shirt will help to support the arm in this comfortable position close to the body as you try to find medical attention.

HACK RATING

DIFFICULTY	
USEFULNESS	
COOL FACTOR	

Make a Fish Trap Out of an Empty Bottle

The must know simple and effective fish catching device

You have probably seen many people using a rod and reel when trying to catch a fish. But who packs a fishing rod with reel, tackle, and bait every time they step out the door? Here is a cool trick that, if done well, can help you catch lots of small fish and aquatic life with hardly any effort. All you need is an empty plastic bottle—a 2 ltr bottle works fantastically.

1. Start by taking your knife or cutting tool and carefully cutting the bottle across its width, with the lid end slightly smaller than the bottom end. Also, make a few small holes in the bottom half of the bottle. Take your time; we don't want any accidents at this stage.

2. Now that you have two pieces of the bottle, the next step is to unscrew and remove the bottle cap before pushing the two pieces together, just like in the diagram below. The bottle cap end should be in the middle of the trap.

3. Add some worms or bugs as bait to the trap and a few pebbles to weigh it down in the water. Place the bottle trap in a slack piece of water; the inside of a bend usually works well. The holes allow water to pass through the trap and spread the scent of the bait downstream. The trap works because a small fish will become interested in the bait inside, swim in through the funnel-shaped

opening, but cannot swim back out again. Fish are not intelligent enough to find the small exit hole in the middle you see. Leave the trap for a few hours, and you should have quite the catch when you check it!

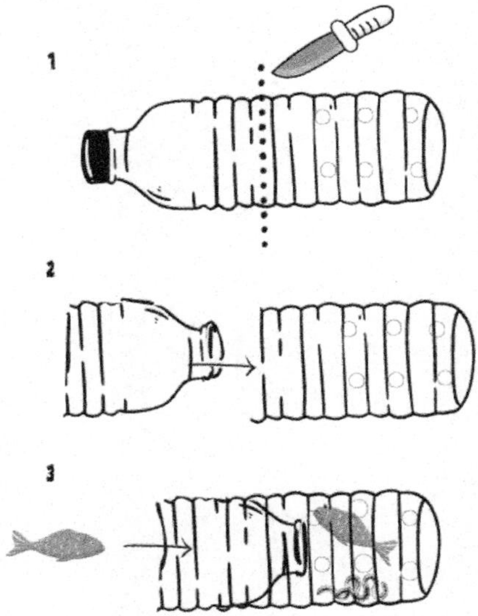

HACK RATING

DIFFICULTY

USEFULNESS

COOL FACTOR

Homemade Compass That Really Works!

No compass, no problem. Learn how to make your own compass in seconds

A compass works by using the earth's magnetic field. The needle on the compass dial is like a small magnet, and when held level, the effect of the earth's magnetic field causes it to point toward 'magnetic north'.

Once you know which direction is north, you can easily work out south, east and west. This means you can navigate from one place to another.

So all you need to make a compass is a piece of magnetised metal and something allowing it to lay horizontally and spin around freely. Here is what you do:

1. Find a sewing needle and rub a magnet backwards and forwards over the sharp, pointy end for about a minute. This will turn the needle into a mini-magnet. Any small, thin piece of metal will do; you can even use a straightened-out paper-clip.

2. Now, suspend the needle in the air by carefully tying a thin piece of string around its centre point. The string should not be twisted or kinked, as this may affect how the needle spins.

3. Now, hold your compass out in front so that the needle lies horizontally. After a few seconds, the needle should come to rest, pointing in the direction of true north.

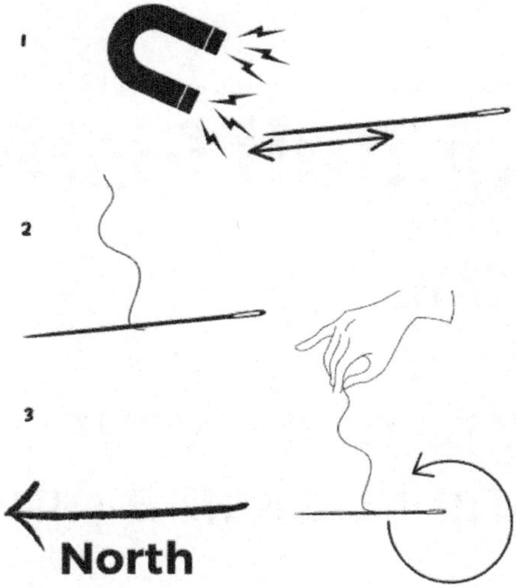

Another way is to rest the magnetised needle on top of a leaf floating on the water's surface. The leaf and water allow the needle to spin freely, and the 'bush compass' will quickly point you in the direction of north. Give it a try; you never know when you may need to use this navigation trick for real.

HACK RATING

DIFFICULTY 

USEFULNESS 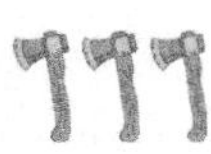

COOL FACTOR 

Ring Pull Fishing Hook

How to make your own fishing hook in a pinch

Probably the most important skill for an accomplished survival expert is the ability to adapt or improvise in any situation. Sometimes, we must make the most of whatever resources and equipment we can scavenge or find in our rucksacks.

Fishing is a great way to catch food in a long-term survival situation; it can keep energy levels high and help maintain performance. But what happens if you do not have a fishing kit? Would you know how to improvise or adapt something that appears completely useless to you in your predicament? Well, after this chapter, you will.

The ring pull from a standard soda can be easily made into an effective fishing hook in seconds. Use the plier on a multitool (everybody should carry a multitool whenever heading out on a hike or wilderness adventure!) to snip the ring pull, as shown in the diagram. If you don't have a tool handy, you can carefully bend the metal backwards and forwards a few times until it breaks, but getting the exact shape you want is more difficult.

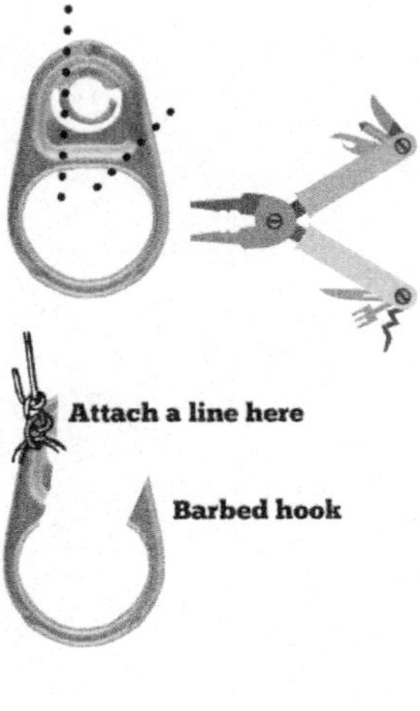

These improvised fishing hooks will be very sharp if made well, so be sure to wear gloves when cutting and handling them to avoid injury.

HACK RATING

DIFFICULTY 

USEFULNESS 

COOL FACTOR 

The Military Method of Waterproofing a Rucksack

The simple way to protect your stash from the wet

Having warm, dry clothes ready to grab from in your bag is crucial when spending time outdoors, especially on cold days and nights. As soon as we stop moving for a while to rest or to go to sleep, the body begins to cool down rapidly. Without the working muscles generating warmth, we need to rely on dry, insulating layers to trap warm air close to the skin. When things get wet, they lose most of their ability to keep up warm and protected. Imagine putting cold, wet pyjamas on and then trying to go to sleep in a damp sleeping bag, it's going to be tough.

There are lots of ways that our clothing and equipment can get wet whilst tucked away in a rucksack. Heavy rainfall can quickly seep through the fabric of a rucksack, especially when there is no cover around to shelter under until it passes. Even laying your bag down on damp ground or wet grass can lead to a soggy sleeping bag in no time. Crossing a river is something that a survivor in the wild may be faced with to get to safety. This method will not only keep your dry layers dry, and even give you a buoyancy aid at the same time.

All you need for this hack is a dry bag. This is a waterproof liner or bag that can be sealed at the top. You can either buy one of these for almost no money online or even cheaper than that, you can just grab a simple garbage bag. The important thing is that it's waterproof. Dry bags are great because you can roll up the top end and click the fastener to seal it. Then when you need to get inside it, just unclip the fastener and unroll to grab your warm and dry jacket. If using a garbage bag, you'll need to tie a knot in the top to seal it, which will work but then can be a pain to open again without damaging the bag.

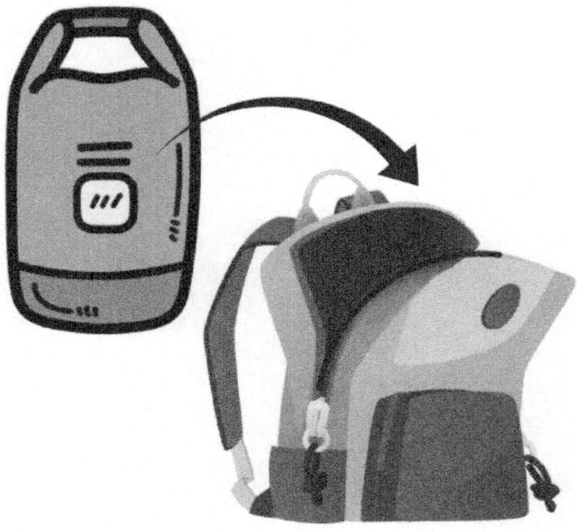

Simply take your empty rucksack and stuff the dry bag or garbage bag inside, with the open end at the top. Now fill your rucksack as normal, but make sure everything goes inside your new waterproof layer. Before you close the top flap on your rucksack, be sure to seal the dry bag. A simple but potentially lifesaving survival tip to make sure your dry layers....stay dry.

HACK RATING

DIFFICULTY 

USEFULNESS 

COOL FACTOR 

How to Make a Bed in the Wild

The right way to build the perfect forest bed.

Protection is the number one priority if you find yourself in a survival situation. Perhaps you wandered off track whilst out on a hike; it's getting dark, and you finally surrender to the fact that you're going to have to spend the night in the wilderness. You're unlikely to have a sleeping mat with you; therefore, you will need to make your bed using the resources you can find close by.

The most important job of our makeshift bed is that it lifts and insulates us away from the cold ground. Laying directly on the ground is not a great way to preserve body heat, and you could quickly be battling mild hypothermia. Instead, it would help if you created a pocket of air between you and the ground to trap some of the warmth that your body is producing.

Depending on how much time you have, there are two options here:

1. **The Futon Method** – All you need to do here is make a mattress on the ground out of dry, leafy branches and vegetation. Gather up as much of this thick, springy vegetation as you can find and lie it down where you plan to sleep. Aim for a thickness of roughly 'fist to elbow' or approximately 45cm for an adult. Use anything sharp and spiky, such as Holly, as a bottom layer before adding softer branches and leaves to the middle and top. Now, when you lie down for some much-needed sleep, the small air gaps between the layers of vegetation will provide insulation away from the cold earth, keeping you much warmer than a night spent on the ground. If spending multiple nights on your makeshift bed,

you should replace the vegetation with new each day, as your weight will compress the layers as you rest, making it less effective next time.

2. **The Cowboy Bed** – Now, if you have some time and a folding saw or other cutting tool, you could make yourself a more permanent wild bed. You can create a bed frame that lifts you up and away from the ground using a few thick branches. Once you have the frame, add layers of dry, leafy vegetation, just like with the futon bed, to create a little more warmth and comfort. Start by placing a couple of logs about 10 cm thick and 50 cm long on the ground; these are the legs of your bed. Then, place some long, straight branches over the legs to create the bed slats. Add as many as you like until you feel it's wide enough. Stake some smaller sticks into the ground up against the outside of your bed frame to stop it from moving. Now you have a fantastic bed frame to add your 'survival mattress' of vegetation.

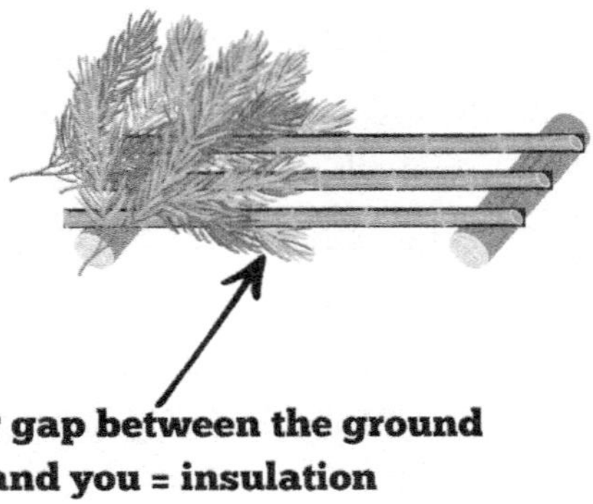

Remember, you need insulation from the cold ground when sleeping outdoors. Building a cowboy bed with a leafy mattress is the next best thing if you don't have a camping mat.

HACK RATING

DIFFICULTY

USEFULNESS

COOL FACTOR

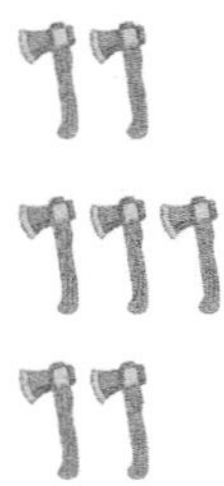

Super Lip Balm Fire Starter

This crazy hack makes starting a fire too easy

A small lip balm stick or tin can be a great addition to your survival kit. It can help soothe dry or sore lips, especially in cold weather. But it's also worth noting that many lip balm products are made with petroleum jelly, which is essentially the same substance used as fuel for motor vehicles like cars or trucks. This makes these lip balm products flammable and something that we can use in an emergency to help start a fire.

Petroleum jelly is ideally used as an 'extender' when lighting a fire. An extender is a highly flammable substance that will burn for a long time, giving your fire every chance of success and becoming self-sustaining.

To use lip balm as an extender:

1. Prepare the base for your fire, and gather up all of your dry tinder into a pile.

2. Take a blob of the lip balm and place it into your

tinder bundle.

3. Go ahead and light your tinder. You will notice that the blob of lip balm will ignite and burn with a cloud of thick, black smoke. Keep adding dry, thin twigs on top of the flame.

4. The flame from the petroleum jelly extender will last for around 45-60 seconds, depending on how much you apply. This should be plenty of time for you to establish a roaring fire.

The lip balm fire starter hack is a great way to make lighting a fire in the wild super-easy.

HACK RATING

DIFFICULTY 

USEFULNESS 

COOL FACTOR 

How to Clean Your Teeth in the Wild

Keeping your mouth healthy with no toothbrush

With the excitement of packing for an adventure, it can be easy to forget some of the essential items that we use every day like a toothbrush or toothpaste. If you find yourself in the wilderness without these bathroom staples, you may need to adapt materials around you that can do the same job.

First, you will need to find a thin hardwood branch to make a toothbrush. Hardwood trees include Oak, Hazel and Ash, to name a few. Cut or snap off a thin part of a branch similar in size to a regular manual toothbrush. Once you have selected your branch, using your fingers, begin to split and fray the fibres at one end. When they start to look like a paintbrush, safely cut them into one straight line. Use your saliva to soften the fibres into bristles by gently chewing on the stick, allowing the 'brush-end' to look more and more like a conventional toothbrush or paintbrush.

Now that you have a working-nature toothbrush, you can go one further and make some natural toothpaste. By grinding down pieces of charcoal from a campfire with rocks and mixing it with some drinking water, it's possible to make a fine paste which will remove impurities from your pearly whites. However, always make sure that the charcoal you're using is safe and that you know where it has come from. Also, be sure to remove any sandy or gritty material from the charcoal, as this will cause damage to the enamel on your teeth.

HACK RATING

DIFFICULTY

USEFULNESS

COOL FACTOR

Lost tent pegs? No problem!

Make a natural tent peg in 60 seconds.

Whether it's securing your tarp correctly to keep the rain off your head, or pitching a tent before hitting the sleeping mat for some well-earned rest, you will need strong, reliable tent pegs. Tent pegs help to secure the guy lines to the ground, allowing you to tension the fabric of your shelter and hold everything in place. Some problems with tent pegs are that they are easy to misplace, lose or break. So what can you do if you find yourself in a fix and need extra tent pegs?

1. Cut a strong, live branch about 6 inches long with a natural hook. It should resemble a Nike swoosh sign.

2. Carefully sharpen the end without the natural hook with a knife or axe. This will make it easier to stake into the ground.

3. Drive your new tent peg into the ground at a 45-degree angle, pointing away from your guy line.

Now you know how to make a spare tent peg if needed, and you can rest easy knowing that your tent or tarp is safely attached to the ground on a windy evening.

HACK RATING

DIFFICULTY 

USEFULNESS 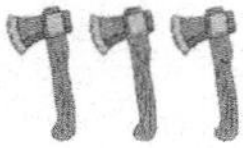

COOL FACTOR 

How to Make a Working Outdoor Shower

Keep clean and refreshed anywhere, anytime

If you spend enough time in the wilderness, you will soon find it easy to get dirty. Sweating all day long, sleeping on the ground, and rummaging around in the undergrowth means that personal hygiene is something you need to take seriously. Taking a shower can be the most refreshing and fantastic feeling when you're feeling smelly and gross, but what happens if you are miles away from civilisation? Here is a neat trick you can try to construct a working, warm water shower in the wild using only a large plastic container:

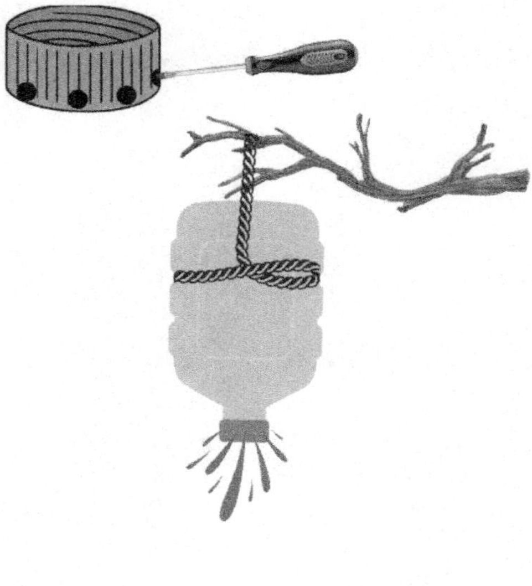

1. Remove the screw top from your container and pierce a few holes around the inside, above the highest thread line.

2. Go ahead and fill the container with clean, safe

water and tightly re-screw the lid back on.

3. If you turn the bottle upside down, no water should come out. If it does, the holes are too large or not in the right place. Attach some cordage to the container and hang it upside down from a tree in direct sunlight.

4. Allow the sun to warm the water for a few hours. When you're ready for shower time, gently un-screw the lid until water begins to spray out.

Once the water has run out, refill the container with water and place it back into direct sunlight, ready for your next wild shower.

HACK RATING

DIFFICULTY 

USEFULNESS 

COOL FACTOR 

Navigation Using Only the Stars

No compass, no problem....but only if you have the skills!

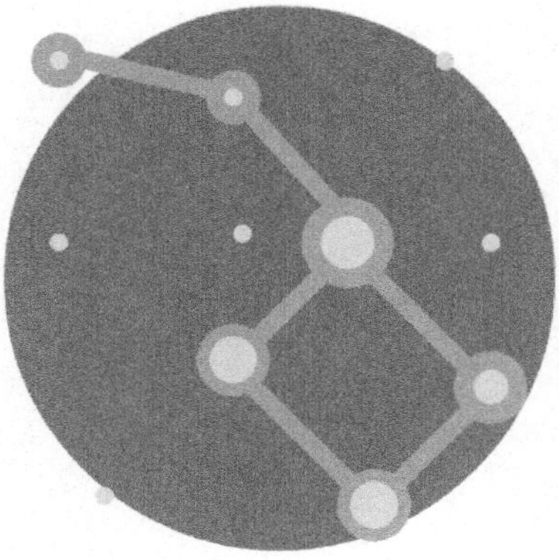

Our ancestors have used the stars for thousands of years to travel the world. Before maps and GPS, sailors and nomadic tribes worked out that certain formations of stars in the night sky could help show the direction of travel. A specific group of stars is called a constellation, and there are many in the sky. Only a few of them will help us find north or south. Once you know which direction north is, working out the other main cardinal points of south, east, and west is easy.

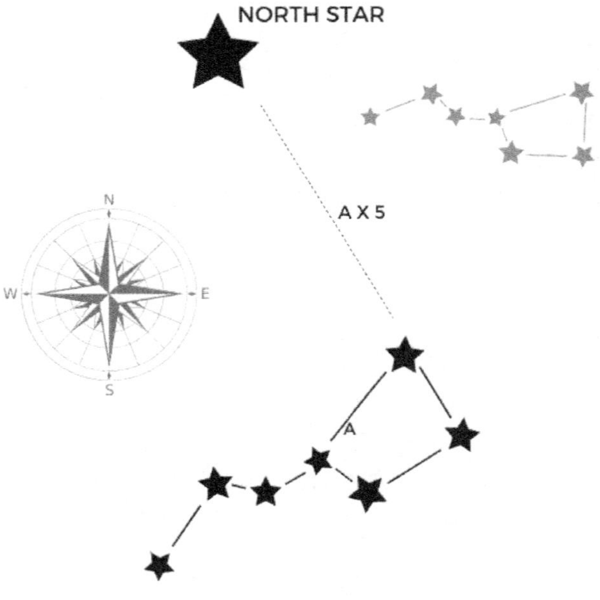

The Big Dipper:

This constellation is also known as 'The Plough' due to its distinctive shape. These stars form part of a larger constellation called Ursa Major. The long handle and bowl shape resemble a saucepan, which is a great way of recognising it among the many other stars in the sky. The two 'pointer' stars on the far right edge of the illustration above lead you straight to Polaris, also called the North Star, if you draw a line straight through them. Remember, the North Star is **NOT** the brightest star in the sky, as some people believe. Polaris sits right above Earth's north-south axis, which is why it doesn't appear to move across the night sky like the other stars. Therefore, if we are looking at the North Star, then we are always facing true north.

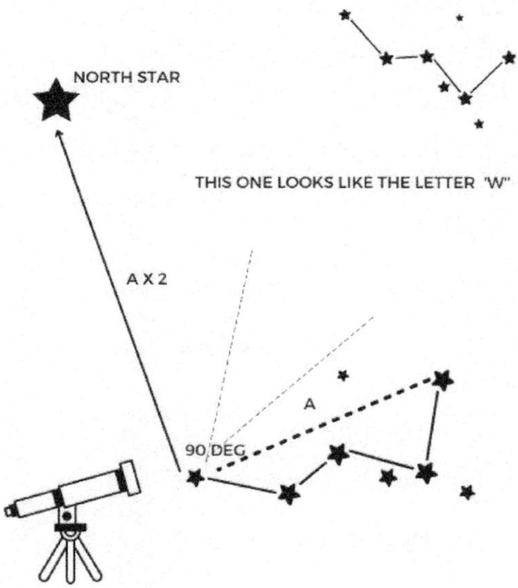

Cassiopeia:

Cassiopeia is another great way to find a direction on a clear night. Just like with Ursa Major, we use this constellation to find the North Star and work out the rest from there. Cassiopeia looks like the letter 'W' in the sky and is again very recognisable once you are familiar with it. To use this group of stars, draw an imaginary line between the furthest two points of the 'W', turn it through 90 degrees and double this length, and you will have Polaris or the North Star.

Now you know two constellations that will help you find north without a compass or technology. If you're in the northern hemisphere and it's a clear night this evening, see if you can find both of them and pinpoint the north star.

HACK RATING

DIFFICULTY

USEFULNESS

COOL FACTOR

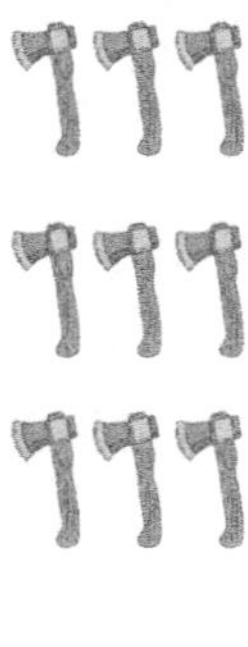

How to Eat an Insect

All you need to know about this amazing survival snack?

For years, many countries worldwide have used insects as a food source. Now, some people in the modern Western world may think it's disgusting to chew on a deep-fried tarantula or nibble on a grasshopper lollipop, but these foods are like candy to many people.

As a matter of fact, insects can be a fantastic source of protein and other nutrients if you know which to eat and how to prepare them properly. Feasting on insects rather than the usual pigs and cows is much better for the planet, as it's far more sustainable.

Here is a list of typical insects that make excellent survival food:

- Grasshoppers and crickets
- Earthworms
- Grubs and maggots
- Ants
- Woodlice
- Scorpions (only in an emergency, they're dangerous!)

ALWAYS cook an insect before eating – this removes any parasites that could make you sick.

DO NOT eat something that is brightly coloured; it's a natural warning sign to stay away!

How to cook an insect:

For an insect with a hard exoskeleton like a **cricket**, you need to grip it firmly, twist it, and pull the head off, followed by the back legs (these contain sharp barbs that can get stuck in the throat). Then, pop it onto a stick and toast it over a flame for a few seconds.

For **grubs, worms**, and other slow-moving creatures, roast them in a hot pan for a few minutes to cook them thoroughly and kill any parasites.

Ants and **woodlice** can be boiled for a few minutes before eating. When they're ready, the woodlice bellies should go white. Bon appetite!

HACK RATING

DIFFICULTY 

USEFULNESS 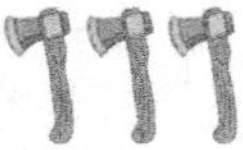

COOL FACTOR 

How to Stop a Nettle Sting From Hurting

The easy to find super-weed that actually works!

Perhaps one of the greatest lies we are told as kids is that the painful throb of a stinging nettle sting can be fixed by rubbing a dock leaf on the area. If you're not sure what a dock leaf is, it's a broad, green-leafed plant that grows almost everywhere, particularly near patches of stinging nettles. When you accidentally brush against a stinging nettle, you quickly get the unmistakable sharp, burning pain caused by tiny, needle-shaped hairs injecting a cocktail of different chemicals into the skin. Parents use the placebo effect of rubbing a dock leaf onto the affected area to calm children down, but there is no scientific reason why this plant could be effective in easing the nettle's sting. A placebo effect is when a person believes in something so much that the body is tricked into thinking it has worked.

To treat a nettle sting for real, you should seek out a weed-looking plant called plantain. Plantain contains antihistamines and other properties that can reduce inflammation and even fight bacterial infections, as well as vitamins and minerals. You can eat plantain if you're hungry, but to use it as a medicine for a sting, chew the leaf up in your mouth for a few seconds before rubbing the paste, or 'poultice', onto the red and hurting area. Within a minute or two, you should notice the symptoms of the stinging nettle gradually reducing.

Learn how to spot plantain.

Plantain comes in several different forms, with Ribwort Plantain being the easiest to recognise. Its long green oval-shaped leaves have a 'ribbed' or striped appearance. The flower head is long and thin and grows from the stem. See if you can spot this super-plant the next time you're wandering around near grassy fields.

Although the plant is perfectly edible, it doesn't taste that great. Imagine if the colour green had a taste—this would be that very taste! The plant is most widely used for its amazing superpowers of healing and makes a brilliant resource for anyone in a survival situation. If there were ever a zombie apocalypse, with food and medicine hard to find, then ribwort plantain could prove to be extremely useful.

HACK RATING

DIFFICULTY

USEFULNESS

COOL FACTOR

Turn your Watch into a Compass

Got a watch but no compass?....this cool trick will help you find direction.

Navigation is one of the key skills you need when moving around in the outdoors. You may be lost and trying to make your way back to a town or road, or you may have taken a hike through the mountains and want to head towards a beautiful lake. Knowing which cardinal direction to head, such as north, south, east, or west, is normally a good start. Without a compass to guide you, it's not always easy to know which direction is which.

Did you know that you can use the hands and face of your normal analogue watch to determine the cardinal direction? It's a quick and dirty way of finding north, south, east, and west if you're in the northern hemisphere. It's not something to use instead of a good compass, but if you're in a fix and have nothing else, it's a great trick to know.

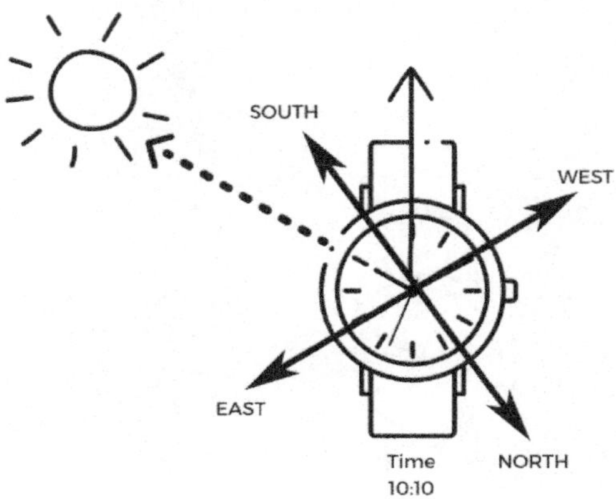

To find direction using a watch face:

- Hold the watch out in front in the palm of your hand so it lies flat or parallel to the ground. Turn your body so the hour hand points in the same direction as the sun.

- Now, draw an imaginary line that goes straight up through the centre of 12 on your watch.

- With your watch in this position, the line midway between the hour hand and 12 o'clock is the direction towards the south.

- Now that you know where south is, it's easy to figure out the other cardinal points from there.

Now you know how it works, see if you can figure out the cardinal points of the example below:

This neat survival hack will help you stay on course without a compass or fancy GPS system. It gives you a good estimate of the cardinal points but should not be used instead of a real compass.

Give it a try the next time you're outside. Once you think you've worked out where north or south is, use a compass to check that you're right!

HACK RATING

DIFFICULTY 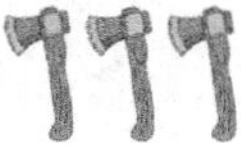

USEFULNESS 

COOL FACTOR 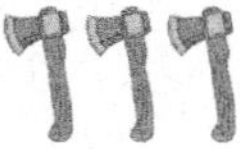

How to Make a Natural Shelter in the Woods

Who needs a tent....build your own sanctuary in the woods

Surviving a night in the woods can be pretty scary. Now imagine you have no shelter, no place to keep you safe and dry. You have no tent, no tarp, absolutely nothing. Well, to make your situation a little better, you could spend some time making yourself a natural shelter. Protection from the environment is the **first priority of survival**, so it's important to act quickly in the daytime before it gets too dark, cold and miserable.

The concept of a 'lean-to' shelter is quite simple: find two trees that are around one and a half times your body length away from each other where the ground is nice and flat. Now, all you need is a long branch that you can use as a cross-bar to span between the two trees. With your crossbar in place, lay smaller branches over the back of your shelter from the crossbar down to the ground. These are called ribs and give the roof of your shelter a skeleton structure.

The next thing you need to do is thatch the frame of your roof with thick, lush vegetation to protect you from the wind and rain. The cut end of your branch should rest against your crossbar so that any water that hits the back of your shelter will run away down the curves of the leaves or pine needles. Keep layering the leafy branches onto your roof until you can barely see any daylight coming through.

Once you have finished your roof, the shelter is ready to be used. To make it even more comfortable, you could make a bed out of spare leafy branches by piling them up into a makeshift mattress around 30cm deep. Lifting yourself up from the floor like this is a great way to stay a little warmer through the night. A small campfire that is a safe distance from where you're sleeping would also help keep you toasty warm while keeping unfriendly animals and insects away.

Have a go at building your very own lean-to shelter the next time you are in the woods. You never know; you might have to build one in a real survival situation one day!

HACK RATING

DIFFICULTY 

USEFULNESS 

COOL FACTOR 

Eating a Fish Caught in the Wild

How to prepare the fish you've just caught

Catching a fish in the wild is a wonderful skill to have if you are in a wilderness survival situation. Even in normal daily life, lots of people enjoy heading to the river or shoreline to make the catch of the day, feeding themselves and their families. In many countries, it is the job of the children in the family to not only catch fish from the river using large fishing nets but also to prepare those fish for the fire or cooking pot.

Fish contain fats, protein, and minerals, which are incredibly valuable to somebody who is in a survival situation. Compared to other animals like rabbits or birds, fish are pretty easy to catch if you have some basic fishing kit and a little skill. You should always cook a fish before you eat it, as they can carry parasites. Boiling the fish in water is the best way to save all the calories and goodness the fish provides, but they also taste great grilled over a fire.

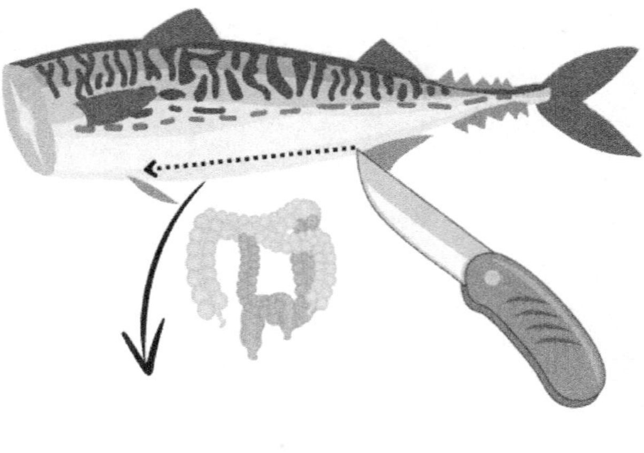

Here's what you need to do to prepare your freshly caught fish so it's ready to cook and eat:

1. Carefully slice open the belly of the fish, going from the tail up towards the neck. Use your knife upside down to cut 'upwards' so that you don't puncture the guts of the fish.

2. Use your fingers to scrape out the insides of the fish until only an empty cavity remains.

3. You can remove the fins and tail if you like, but be careful of the sharp spines that some fish have within their fins.

Now, your fish is ready to eat, so go ahead and grill it over an open flame or wrap it in foil and slowly roast it on the coals. Delicious!!

HACK RATING

DIFFICULTY 

USEFULNESS 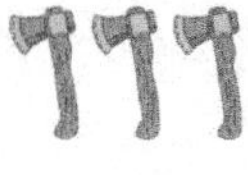

COOL FACTOR 

Make Fire With a Bottle of Water

Sounds crazy right, but it works!

Have you ever used a magnifying glass or fresnel lens to burn a hole into paper or a leaf? Perhaps you have seen someone else do it. The lens of the magnifying glass focuses the light rays and energy from the sun into a small area, which gets really hot. From there, it is simple to focus this small area on some tinder and start a fire using only the sun's energy.

If you have a clear plastic bottle with a smooth, rounded bottom, you can use the exact same principle to focus the sun's rays and create a hot spot. The round bottom of the clear plastic bottle acts like a lens, and as light passes through it, you can tilt and adjust it to create a tiny hot spot that will set fire to some tinder. Full disclosure—it's not easy and takes lots of patience with a steady hand, but with practice, it's totally achievable. Here's what you need to do:

1. Quarter-fill your clear plastic bottle with water

and hold it 1-2 inches from the ground.

2. Start by tilting the bottle to about 45 degrees and see if you can find the beam of light that passes through it and onto the ground.

3. The aim is to make the patch of light shining through the bottle as small as possible. To do this, slowly tilt and move the bottle around.

4. To build up the heat, hold your small light spot on dark-coloured tinder, like brown paper or coffee grounds, until you see it begin to smoke and char. Pretty soon, you can add cotton wool or wood shavings to create a fire.

Being able to make a fire is an important survival skill, but remember to get someone responsible to supervise you if you are practising fire lighting techniques.

HACK RATING

DIFFICULTY 

USEFULNESS 

COOL FACTOR 

Extreme Environments

Survive a Fall Onto Subway Tracks

How to deal with
this urban underground
danger

Subway and Tube stations are amazing feats of human engineering. They were built to keep us mobile and connected anywhere in the city we'd like to go. The fact that these stations are deep underground can be scary enough for some people, with endlessly long sets of stairs that lead you into a dark, gloomy new world beneath the streets.

Someone who has a deep fear of small spaces, a 'claustrophobe', may also find subways scary places to be. Their long, narrow, dark tunnels and tightly packed train carriages during rush hour can be a real challenge. However, there is another hazard in the subway that many people fear the most: falling onto the railway tracks! With its high, steep walls, there is little chance for an average person to be able to climb back onto the platform above without some help. When a train does come along, most lines only have a tiny gap between the speeding juggernaut and the safety of the platform.

In the movies, we often watch a secret agent chase after a bad guy as they both disappear into the darkness beyond the platform. Normally, a speeding train appears in the distance, ready to splat anything in its way. Quite often, the hero will dive into a small gap in the wall at the very last minute to avoid becoming a bug on the train's windscreen. But how realistic is this? Let's find out.

Here is what you should do if you fall from the platform at a subway station:

1. **A Helping Hand** – The best way to get out of your sticky situation is to shout for help and hope that someone can pull you back up before the next train comes along. Grab each other's wrists, jump, and as you reach the highest point of the jump, try to throw your opposite leg over the platform edge.

2. **Get Between The Tracks** – If the station you are at has two sets of tracks, each running in opposite directions, quickly move to the gap between them on seeing a train approaching. This should give you enough space to avoid getting hit. Just watch for any mirrors or other objects sticking out from the carriages.

3. **Look For Spaces** – On most lines, there will be small spaces underneath the platform used for general maintenance that you may be able to squeeze into if a train is fast approaching. Just be sure the space is deep enough that your body doesn't push past the platform's edge.

4. **Last Resort** – If you have tried everything else and had no luck, lie as flat as you can in the centre of the tracks and hope the train passes over you.

This is only to be done as a last resort when all other efforts to get away from the oncoming train have failed.

HACK RATING

DIFFICULTY 

USEFULNESS 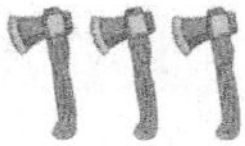

COOL FACTOR 

Identify a Poisonous Animal

Spot the warning signs early to stay safe

Nature has developed excellent ways to warn people that an animal is toxic and likely to cause serious harm if it is tampered with. Some animals produce a toxin that's 1,200 times more poisonous than cyanide! Therefore, it's important to know these warning signs so that we can quickly identify that the animal is dangerous and keep a safe distance.

Like humans, animals must be able to protect themselves from other animals that may wish to eat them. Having toxic weaponry, such as a venomous bite or poisonous tissue, helps the animal become less appetizing to predators.

Poisonous animals – have toxins on their skin or tissues designed to kill anything that touches or eats them. An example is the poison dart frog of South America and the Cane toad

Venomous animals – have specialised glands which produce venom that's delivered to the prey using fangs (snake/spider) or stingers (jellyfish/lionfish)

So, how do you spot a venomous or poisonous animal?

BRIGHTLY COLOURED

If a creature has obvious, contrastingly bright colouration, it is a classic sign that warns predators it is not to be messed with. This phenomenon is called *aposematic colouration* and is found in poisonous frogs and some marine life. The highly venomous black widow spider has a bright red patch on its back, which is another example of this.

PRODUCE A STRANGE NOISE

The 'rattle' of a Diamondback Rattlesnake is an unmistakable audible warning sign to anyone coming a little too close to this highly venomous snake of North America. This animal has evolved an excellent warning sign for anyone who is walking through the wilderness and about to step on or near this creature.

FURRY INSECTS

Some species of poisonous caterpillars pack a nasty punch if touched or eaten. The Furry Puss Caterpillar looks pretty harmless, but tiny barbs along its body can deliver a painful sting, resulting in skin blistering and severe pain. Although we can eat many types of insects, if something is hairy or particularly furry, then it should be avoided.

Surviving Cold Water Shock

Sudden cold water immersion can be fatal, learn how to react the right way

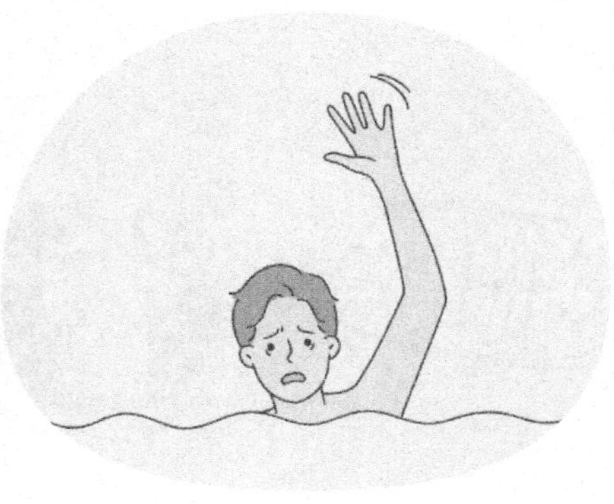

If somebody creeps up behind you and pours a cup of ice-cold water down your neck, what do you think your reaction would be? You'd gasp for air right?! You'd panic, start jumping around and generally be in shock. Well, the body reacts in the same way when suddenly plunged into cold water, and we call this phenomenon 'cold water shock'. It's the main cause of hundreds of fatalities around the world each year.

The sudden, deep inhalation of breath is called the *gasp reflex,* and if your head is under the water when it occurs, can cause you to drown. So, what do you need to remember to do if this happens to you?

1. **Stay Calm** – Try to resist the urge to panic. This is not helpful. Instead, you must stay calm and relaxed for a few seconds as the initial cold wa-

ter shock passes and your breathing returns to a steady state again. Floating on your back with your nose and mouth above the water may help this. Eventually, your body will get used to the change in temperature. Remove any heavy, baggy clothing to help you stay afloat.

2. **Assess**—Now that you have regained your composure and are no longer gasping for air, try to tread water and look around for something you can hold onto or swim towards. If you think people may be close by, start shouting for help as loudly as you can.

3. **Move with purpose, but don't rush** – If you can swim towards safety, do so in a controlled way using a simple 'doggy paddle' or backstroke movement. If you swim frantically, you could quickly become out of breath, exhausted and in big trouble again.

HACK RATING

DIFFICULTY

USEFULNESS

COOL FACTOR

Surviving a Fall Through the Ice

When walking on ice goes very wrong!

The best way to prevent a fall through the ice is to avoid walking on it. Even if you are sure the water is not deep, or the ice looks super thick and strong, only venture over a frozen river or lake if you absolutely must.

Every year, hundreds of people are unlucky enough to experience a fall through the ice, and while most can live and tell the tale, unfortunately, many are lost.

At the start of this chapter, we talked about cold water shock and how our bodies can respond when we suddenly find ourselves deep in freezing cold water. Can you remember the 'gasp reflex'? Well, the same thing happens when you fall through the ice. There is a big gasp for air right away as the body struggles to deal with the sudden drop in temperature. The problem worsens if our head is below the water's surface, as water can then get into the lungs.

I've fallen through thin ice.......what should you do?

1. **Don't panic**—it's easier said than done, but if you

think back to cold water shock, it's essential to keep calm and try to control your breathing. After a minute or less, your breathing rate should return to normal. This will help you think clearly about what you need to do next.

2. **Ditch the weight** – quickly remove any heavy rucksacks or bags you may be wearing. Don't waste time trying to remove coats or other items of clothing. Waterproof jackets, for example, are great at trapping tiny pockets of air to help keep you afloat.

3. **Pull yourself out -** If you have ice picks, use them to clear your upper body of the water first, followed by your torso, abdomen, and legs. If you don't have picks, try using your forearms and elbows in the same way.

4. **Lie flat as a pancake**. Do not stand up straight away. Instead, spread your weight evenly over a large area by lying flat, and then slowly roll yourself away from the hole in the ice. Once you feel the ice below is stronger, slowly get to your feet and walk back to safety, warmth, and medical help.

Now that you have survived the ordeal of falling through the ice, you must get somewhere safe, remove all that wet clothing, and get warm quickly. If you don't, hypothermia will set in, and you'll be in just as much trouble!

HACK RATING

DIFFICULTY 

USEFULNESS 

COOL FACTOR 

How to Treat Frostbite

Make sure you don't lose your fingers or toes

Frostbite is most common in the extremities, including the fingers, toes, nose, and ears. It happens when you expose these areas to cold temperatures for long periods. The time it takes to develop frostbite will depend on how extreme the cold is. For example, in high arctic areas, it's possible to succumb to frostbite within only a few minutes, whereas in less severe temperatures, it could be a few hours.

Frostbite causes damage to the nerves, blood vessels, and cells below the surface layer of the skin. If left untreated for long enough, it can lead to amputation of the affected areas. You will often see brave polar explorers on TV with missing fingers or bright red, rosy cheeks due to this condition. So, what signs do we need to look out for to ensure we don't fall foul of frostbite when out on our next off-grid adventure?

- Numbness or loss of feeling in the area
- The skin has a pale white, waxy appearance
- The skin feels hard. That's because the cells are beginning to freeze!

Prevention is better than the cure!

To protect yourself from developing frostbite, limit the time you spend outside in icy conditions. If you need to be outside for a longer period, ensure you have the correct layers of warm clothing, good-quality thick gloves and socks, and a waterproof outer layer to stop you from getting wet. Your skin will lose heat from your body 25 times faster if wet!!

Treatment

So what should you do if you think you or someone you're with has frostbite?

- Get out of the cold! Remove the person to a warmer place.

- Remove wet clothing, socks or gloves and replace them with dry, warm things.

- It is vital to slowly and gently re-warm the area. Submerging it in warm (not hot) water or placing it into the armpits of a kind person works amazingly well. Don't place the hands next to fire; you could cause burns and more damage if the skin is numb.

- Once the area is thawed and has a more red colour, wrap it in clean bandages and try to find medical help.

HACK RATING

DIFFICULTY 

USEFULNESS 

COOL FACTOR 

Finding Water in the Desert

Separate the desert myths from the hard facts

In a desert survival situation, having access to clean, safe drinking water is crucial. Most people need around 6-8 pints of water each day in normal conditions and doing regular, daily things. In a hot desert, where temperatures reach over 100 degrees, this figure increases to around pints or 2 gallons of water.....per day!

The reason we need so much water in the desert is that the body loses lots of it through sweat as it fights to keep us cool and prevent overheating.

Ration Your Sweat!

Reduce the loss of precious water by following these simple tips:

- Only move during the night and cooler parts of the day.
- Find shade and stay there during the hottest part of the day.
- Remove layers of clothing before you start to sweat.

Run out of water? Then you'll need to find some. Here are a few great places to start:

1. **Shady areas below a rock face or cliff**—Water can sometimes sit for weeks in small, hidden pockets at the base of rocky areas, away from the sun's hot rays. Due to gravity, water can also seep through the rocks down towards a lower collection point.
2. **Hollows in trees**—Sometimes, larger trees have

roots that push above the ground, forming little bowls or hollows. These can be great places to find small pockets of water that have not evaporated yet.

3. **Bends in dry river beds**—If you dig down into the earth around the bend of a dried-up river, especially where the bank overhangs slightly above, causing some shade, you may be lucky and find water not too deep below the surface.

4. **An area of lush vegetation**—If plants and trees grow in a particular area of desert, it's a good sign that water is present. It may be hidden underground, but it is worth spending some time exploring and digging around.

5. **Insects and animal tracks** – A good sign of nearby water is seeing lots of insects buzzing around. Insects love to be near water; you could be close to a small pond or puddle full of water. Larger animals walk to and water daily, so look for signs of animals moving in one direction through the undergrowth.

Does a Cactus Hold Water?

Well, it's a living plant, so yes. However, do not be fooled into thinking it's a water fountain waiting to be turned on. Pretty much all cactus water will make you seriously ill if you drink it, as the spongy flesh contains alkaloids, which will cause stomach cramps and vomiting. Only the Fishhook Barrel Cactus is considered safe to drink/eat, but it tastes terrible!

HACK RATING

DIFFICULTY 

USEFULNESS 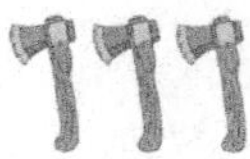

COOL FACTOR 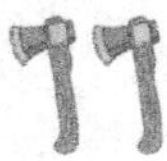

How to Remove a Tick the Right Way

Getting rid of those nasty blood suckers

Ticks are small spider-like parasites that love attaching themselves to unwitting hosts by biting into the skin. A tick is usually tiny, the size of a poppy seed, and the bite is painless, so the host often has no idea that they are carrying this parasitic passenger.

The tick feasts on the host's blood, causing it to increase in size and become more noticeable. Indeed, a tick can often be attached and happily drinking away for hours or days before anyone notices it.

The problem with a tick bite is not the loss of blood; it's that they can pass on Lymes disease, which is a rather unpleasant condition for a human. The chance of contracting Lymes disease from a tick is very low. However, the risk is enough that you should always wear long trousers when hiking through long grass and check yourself, friends and family for ticks regularly if you're living outdoors for any period of time.

How to remove a tick properly:

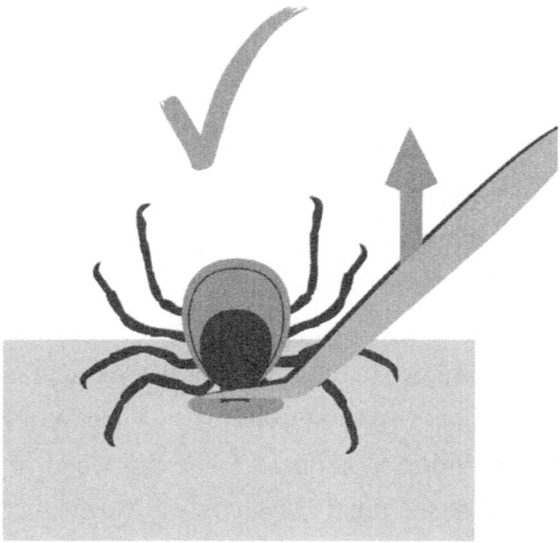

For this job, it's best to use a pair of pointy-end tweezers if you have them. You can also buy a special tick-removing tool which looks like a small plastic hook. These are very handy and should certainly make it into your personal survival tin or adventure first aid kit.

Using tweezers:

- Carefully place the tip of the tweezers between the skin and the ticks head.

- Applying gentle but consistent pressure, slowly lift the tick upwards and away from the skin. Do not twist it; this could cause the head to break away from the body, leaving it inside the skin.

- With steady upward pressure, the tick should release its grip on your skin. Then, you can dispose of it by placing it in some water.

- If the head remains in the skin, try to remove as much as possible using the tweezers before giving the area a good clean using soap and water and/or disinfectant wipes. Do this even if the whole tick comes out nicely.

- Monitor – if a circular rash develops where the tick bit you, or you feel unwell in the next 7-10 days, then see a doctor.

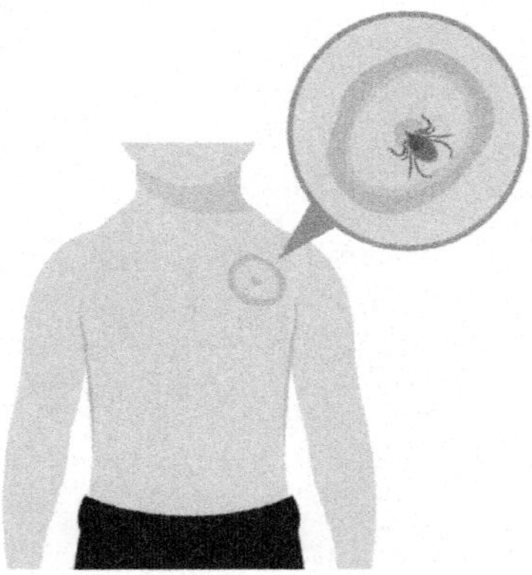

Finding you have a tick somewhere on your body is not uncommon, but it's always best to try and avoid it if possible. Wearing long trousers when walking through long meadows and grassy areas and wearing plenty of insect repellent will certainly help make sure you don't unwittingly become dinner for this tiny parasite passenger.

HACK RATING

DIFFICULTY 

USEFULNESS 

COOL FACTOR 

How to Escape a Rip Current

Dealing with this deadly ocean hazard the right way

Firstly, what is a rip? It's a current that takes water back out to sea after waves have broken onto the shoreline. Rips are very common and are found at most beaches. This is why it's crucial always to swim and surf inside the flags where lifeguards are on duty. These professionals are there to ensure your safety, as rips can swiftly whisk objects away from the shallow water and out to sea, sometimes up to 100 feet or more. If you are a weak swimmer, this can cause panic, fear and sometimes drowning.

Spotting a Rip Current

If you know what to look for, you can easily spot a rip current from the beach and stay well away. Normally, lifeguards will spot this danger first and move everyone away from the area. But, if you are on an unpatrolled beach, you need to be able to identify this hazard yourself, and here's how:

- A channel of rippled water that has smooth water around it.
- Fewer breaking waves in a specific area of the surf.
- Strips of deeper, darker water near the shoreline.
- Floating items like driftwood are being taken out to sea. You might also notice sandy, discoloured water collecting behind the surf.

Dealing With a Rip Current

- DO NOT PANIC! – The current will not pull you under the water, and most people drown from exhaustion from frantically trying to swim against the current back towards the shore. Instead, try swimming sideways across the rip and parallel to the beach until you are free.

- Signal for help – Raise your hands in the air and shout towards the beach. Hopefully, someone will see you and help.

- Just relax – If you're not a good swimmer, float on your back and allow the rip to carry you out to sea. Most rips are less than 100 feet long; sometimes, they take you back to the beach in a big loop.

Now you know how to handle yourself if you get caught up in a rip current at the beach. To stay safe, always swim between the flags at lifeguarded beaches and look for signs of a rip current before entering the water.

HACK RATING

DIFFICULTY 

USEFULNESS 

COOL FACTOR 

Adrift in a Life Raft, Survival at Sea!

How to survive and get rescued if drifting alone at sea

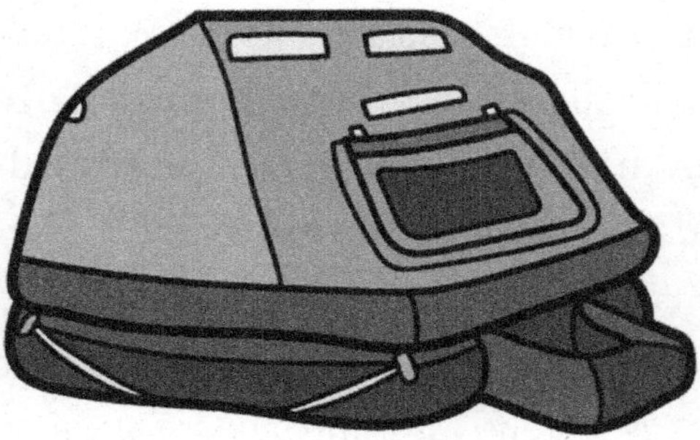

Every day, hundreds of thousands of people fly or sail over the planet's oceans as they effortlessly migrate from one country to the next. What happens if one of those planes suddenly has engine issues and is forced to ditch in the middle of the sea? Luckily, aircraft today are packed with enough life rafts to hold every person on board, keeping them safely out of the water if they need to leave the cabin. Large airliners like the ones that take you on holiday have inflatable slides that passengers can shuffle down, which then become huge floating life rafts.

If you are unfortunate enough to be a lone survivor of a plane crash over water or a shipwreck resulting from a powerful storm, how would you handle yourself? Here are the important things you need to consider:

1. **Protection from the cold**

The first and most crucial thing you must do is remove yourself from the water as quickly as possible. Don't hang around, even if you're wearing a life jacket and in no immediate danger. Each second you spend in the cold water increases the risk of hypothermia. Once your core body temperature of 37 degrees centigrade falls too low, it's hard to recover. If the wind and rain are blowing into your raft, then quickly close and fasten the doors to help you keep warm.

2. Make your new home dry

Most life rafts will have a bailer system on the floor that allows you to empty out any water that might be inside. The last thing you want is to be sitting shivering in a wet raft, so ensuring it's dry is crucial for your comfort and morale. If there is no bailer system, then use anything around that you can scoop water and throw overboard.

3. Signal for help

Check under the seats and storage pockets for any location aids. Items like emergency beacons, flares, and signal mirrors will help the rescue parties find you much faster. Read the instructions printed on each device to help you use it correctly.

4. Keep hydrated

If you're lucky, pouches of emergency drinking water could be stashed in the raft's internal pockets. There could even be a reverse osmosis pump, a clever contraption that turns seawater into drinking water. Think about ways that you could harvest rainwater as it falls from the sky, perhaps using the shelter roof as a huge collection plate.

5. Keep positive

A positive and full-of-grit mindset is needed in any survival situation, and none more than this. The power of the mind cannot be underestimated, and feeding it with the warming thoughts of family and friends who are waiting for you at home can make all the difference to a sole survivor.

HACK RATING

DIFFICULTY 

USEFULNESS 

COOL FACTOR 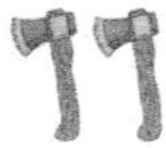

Crossing a Raging River

How to avoid drowning, hypothermia and being swept away!

You might have to cross a river or wide stream for many reasons. Perhaps you're lost out in the wilderness somewhere, and the only thing stopping you from reaching a town or road ahead and safety is the winding, fast-flowing river in front of you. It is important that you know the risks involved with performing a river crossing. It's a key skill that is taught to soldiers worldwide to ensure they can achieve their objectives and missions regardless of whatever obstacles they may face along the way.

You may be alone or in a group; below, you'll find everything you need to make it to the other side safely:

1. **Choose wisely** – Finding the safest place to cross is vital. Try to cross a river at an inside bend, as the water tends to move slower. Always check the river upstream for a shallower, easier place to cross over.

2. **Remove some clothing** – take off your trousers to help reduce the water resistance as you walk through the fast current. This also keeps them dry and ready to put back on after you have crossed. Keep your shoes on to protect your feet from sharp rocks, but remove your socks and keep those dry, too.

3. **Waterproof what you can**— use a plastic or dry bag inside your rucksack to waterproof your spare clothing and fire-lighting equipment. This will be

important when you've made it to the other bank, where you'll probably be cold and wet and need a fire to warm you back up again.

4. **Grab a long stick** – A strong, straight walking pole made from a branch is useful for helping you balance. Enter the water in a shallow part of the river and poke the ground to check the depth before every step.

5. **Face into the current** – **L**ooking upstream, take small, careful steps diagonally as you lean into the stick. Head for a shallow part of the river to exit and watch out for floating debris like logs and trees making their way down the river.

6. **Get dry** quickly—To prevent hypothermia from developing, remove your wet clothes and replace them with dry ones as quickly as possible. Start a small fire using a tinder from your dry rucksack to warm you even quicker if you can.

Crossing in a group

This is the safest way to cross a river. Decide who in the group is the lightest person. Form a chain by linking arms together at the elbow, and ensure the lightest and least confident person is in the middle.

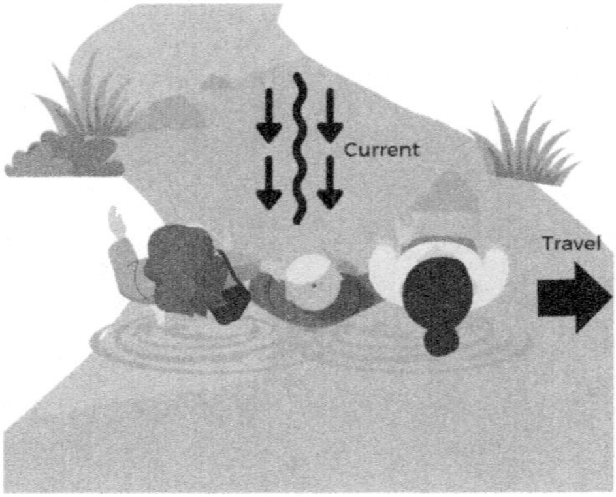

When the group crosses, the strongest person should stand furthest upstream so that he or she can bear the force of the current, with everyone else tucked in below. The group then walks forward in a straight line, keeping this formation as they slowly battle the current until reaching the other side.

HACK RATING

DIFFICULTY 

USEFULNESS 

COOL FACTOR 

Extreme Heat! How to Deal With Heat Stroke

Learn to recognise the signs and treat the symptoms

Having fun in the sun is a great way to spend a hot summer's day. However, you should also be prepared to deal with a medical emergency if the weather is particularly warm. Heat stroke is when the body's core temperature gets too high to keep working properly. As you probably know, the ideal temperature for your body is 37 degrees centigrade, and it has many mechanisms to keep it around that magic number. These mechanisms include sweating, seeking water to drink and pushing the blood to the surface of the skin (like when someone has a red face). It all starts with knowing and recognising some of the signs and symptoms of heat stroke in yourself and others:

- Irritability/being snappy for no reason
- Excessive sweating
- Feeling sick or actually vomiting
- Dizziness or feeling like you're going to faint
- Fast breathing and heart rate
- Muscle cramps in the arms, legs or stomach
- Skin that feels very warm to the touch

But what should you do if you or someone you're with starts showing these symptoms? Heat stroke can be very serious if not dealt with fast and even fatal in some cases, so the important thing is to spot it first and then act quickly. Here are some of the best ways to help someone who you think is suffering from heat stroke:

1. **Call for medical help**. It's better to be safe than sorry; symptoms can worsen quickly.

2. **Remove the person from direct sunshine**. Get them into the shade of a tree or, even better, a building or car with air conditioning. This will help the body begin to cool itself down.

3. **Get rid of any clothing** they don't need to wear,

like jackets or hats. Loosen any tight clothing if you can.

4. **Try giving them a cool drink** to help slowly lower their core body temperature.

5. **Spray with cool water or gently dab them with a wet cloth**. This is the same thing as sweating, which removes heat from the surface of the skin through evaporation.

6. **Stay with them** until more help arrives. Keep talking to the casualty so they feel reassured and less worried by the situation.

Following the emergency first aid listed above can help someone recover from a serious case of heat stroke. The key is to spot the signs early, so be alert and pay attention to those around you and how you feel when outside on a hot day.

HACK RATING

DIFFICULTY 

USEFULNESS 

COOL FACTOR 

Make a Working Log Raft

Float down the river to safety with your own bush-fix log raft

Rivers are like roadways that flow through places like the jungle and mountains. If you are lost in a thick jungle or a mountainous ravine and unsure of which direction to head, following a river can be a great way to find other people and help. Unfortunately, it's usually impossible to walk along a riverbank somewhere like the jungle before the ground becomes too difficult. Therefore, building a log raft to ride down a river could be your only chance of finding a village or nearby help. Making a raft is not all that difficult. All you need to do is collect some floatable materials and have something to lash them together with. Wooden logs work brilliantly for raft building because a) they float, and b) they're easy to find.

What you will need:

- 4-8 logs of roughly the same diameter (depending on how wide you need the raft to be).
- A knife or folding saw
- Some rope or string

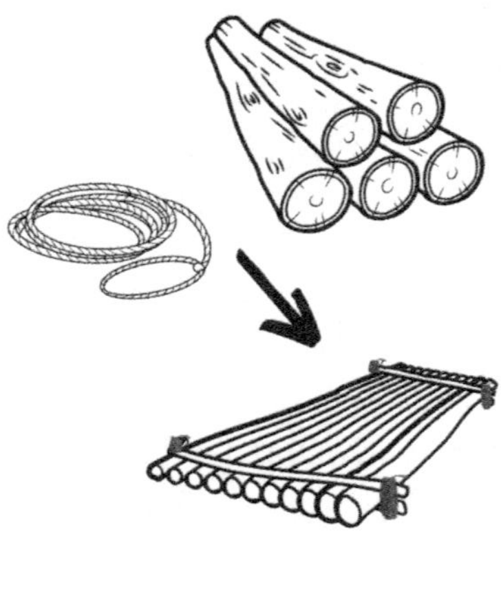

OK, so you have decided that building a log raft is what you must do to find rescue. Follow these simple steps below:

1. Collect some logs that are all roughly the same diameter. Thicker logs will provide more buoyancy but will need more work to cut and find. If the raft is for one person, find thinner logs that don't need cutting and go for these.

2. Lay the logs alongside each other on a flat surface beside the river. Use your knife to cut simple 'V-shaped' notches into either end of the logs. This allows the crosspiece to sit across the main logs snugly.

3. Lash the top and bottom crosspiece logs tightly together. This will hold the logs in place and stop them from drifting apart.

4. Now, you are ready to board your vessel and gently float downstream to safety.

This is a super simple way of making a fully working log raft. Let's hope you never need to make one in a real-life situation, but just in case, now you know how!

HACK RATING

DIFFICULTY 

USEFULNESS 

COOL FACTOR 

Afterword

You've smashed this book out of the park!

Well done, you've now reached the end of this epic guide on how to survive some of the worst situations that nature can throw at you.

You've learnt how to escape a rip current, treat frostbite, make fire with a plastic bottle, navigate using the stars, survive a shark attack and even break down a door – just to name a few things!

I am confident that you now have the mindset, knowledge, and skills to overcome anything that life throws at you.

I hope that you continue to fuel your desire to learn new wilderness survival skills and practice what you've learned.

Keep reading, learning and being curious.

Thankyou

You're a Star

By purchasing this book, you have supported an independent author's journey to create valuable survival guides for young people worldwide.

I would be truly honoured if you would take a moment to leave an honest **review** and share your experience with others. It would mean so much.

Dale

Printed in Great Britain
by Amazon

46140915R00106